MORE

m&m's®

CHOCOLATE CANDIES MATH **BRAND**

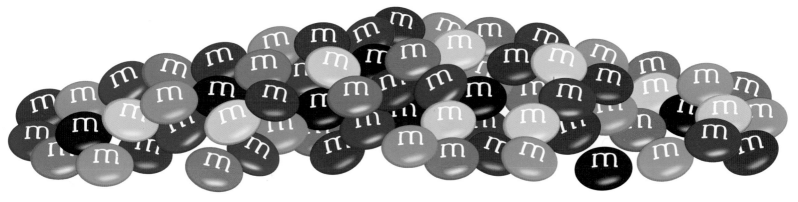

Barbara Barbieri McGrath
Illustrated by Roger Glass

🌉 Charlesbridge

The author would like to thank Donna Armstrong and her fourth grade students at Lilja Elementary School in Natick, Massachusetts, for their assistance and enthusiasm.

Published by Charlesbridge Publishing
85 Main Street, Watertown, MA 02472
(617) 926-0329
www.charlesbridge.com

Library of Congress Cataloging-in-Publication Data
McGrath, Barbara Barbieri, 1954 —
    More M&M's® brand chocolate candies math/by Barbara Barbieri McGrath;
illustrated by Roger Glass.
    p.   cm.
    Summary: Rhyming text and illustrations use candy to teach mathematical skills
and concepts such as estimating, graph interpretation, division, multiplication,
factoring, and problem solving.
    ISBN 0-88106-993-0 (reinforced for library use)
    ISBN 0-88106-994-9 (softcover)
1. Counting—Juvenile literature. 2. Colors —Juvenile literature.
[1. Counting. 2. Color.] I. Glass, Roger, ill.
QA113.M39372   1998
513—dc21   97-29345

Printed in the United States of America
(hc) 10 9 8 7 6 5 4 3 2 1
(sc) 10 9 8 7 6 5 4 3 2 1

The illustrations in this book were done in Macromedia Freehand.
The display type and text type were set in Helvetica and Times.
Color separations were made by Eastern Rainbow Company, Derry, New Hampshire.
Printed and bound by Worzalla Publishing Company, Stevens Point, Wisconsin
Production supervision by Brian G. Walker
Designed by Roger Glass
Computer graphics by Susanne Taylor
This book was printed on recycled paper.

To Albert and Dorothy
        —*B.B.M.*

With love to Di
        —*R.G.*

The exact number of pieces of each color of "M&M's"® Chocolate Candies
may vary from package to package. As a result, there may be insufficient
quantities of each color of "M&M's"® Chocolate Candies in each package
to match the quantity of colors required for play in this book.

Colorful candies will be our counting tools.
Shake them out of the bag, then follow the rules.

Take a quick glance at the total amount.
Keep a guess in your head of how many came out.

Now sort the colors.
How many groups did you get?

We'll use them to count,
so don't eat them just yet.

Let's make a graph
where we'll place all the candy.

For solving math problems,
a graph comes in handy.

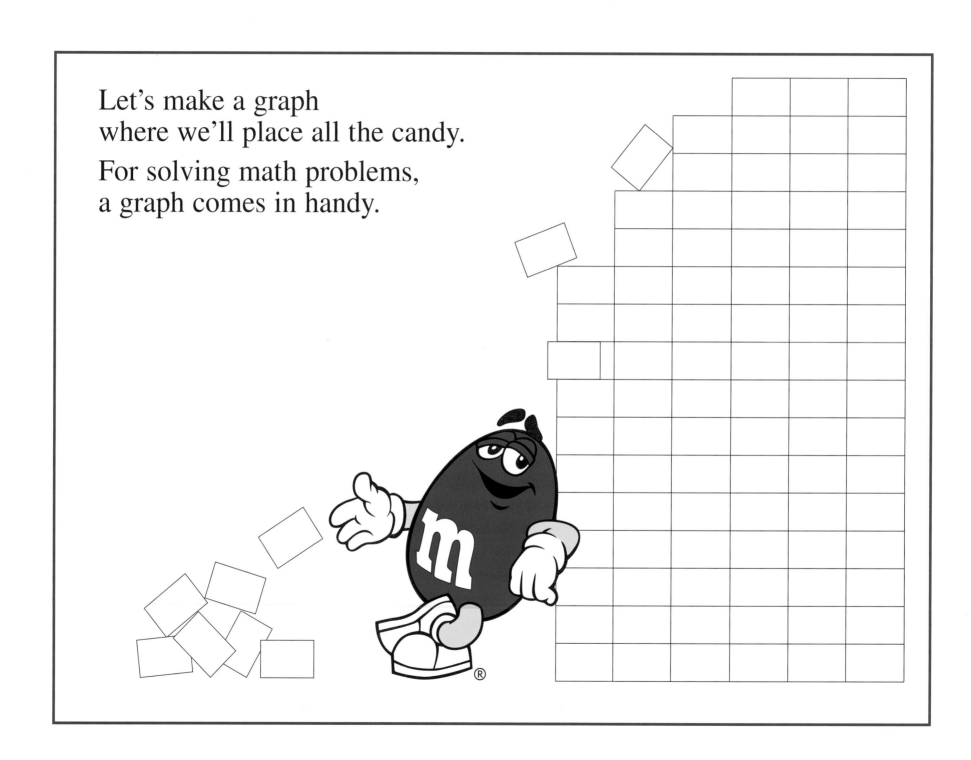

In the row that reads "red,"
place the reds from your pile.

Put one in each box—
this might take a while.

RED	ORANGE	BROWN	BLUE	YELLOW	GREEN
m					
m					
m					
m					
m					
m					
m					
m					
m					
m					

Do the same with the orange, the brown, and the blue.

Don't forget to put yellow and green in there, too.

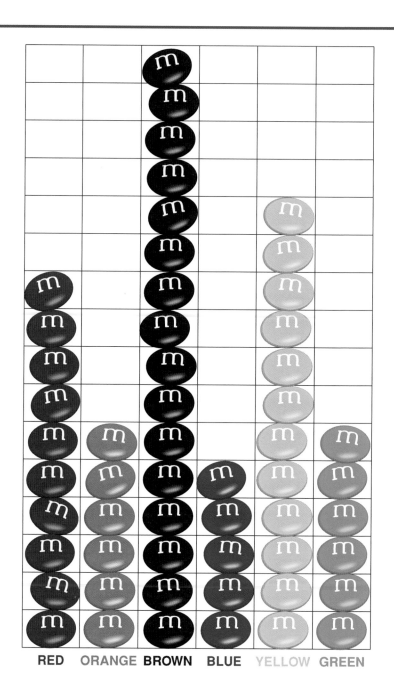

| RED | ORANGE | BROWN | BLUE | YELLOW | GREEN |

Examine the candies
when your hard work has ceased.

Which row has the most?
Which has the least?

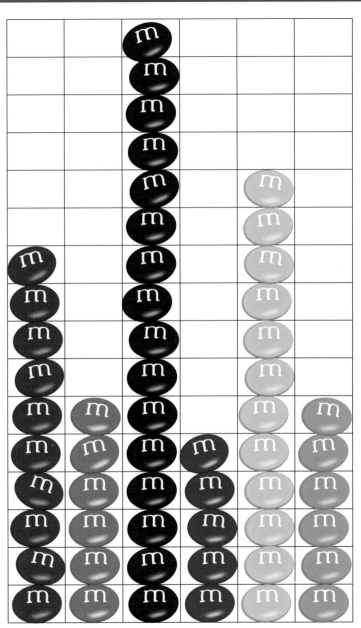

| RED | ORANGE | BROWN | BLUE | YELLOW | GREEN |

Compare the six rows.
Some are short, some are tall.

Are any rows equal?
You make the call.

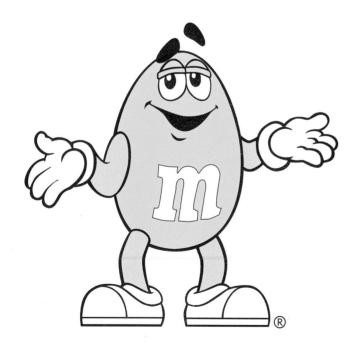

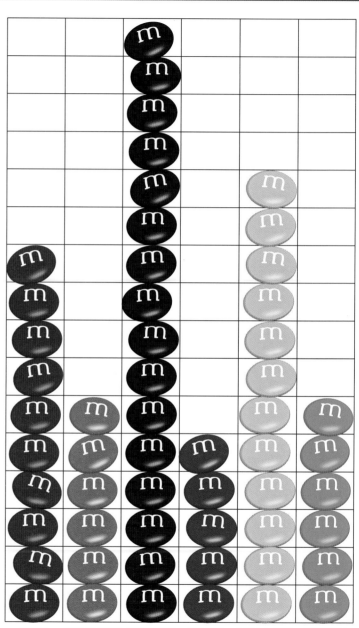

RED   ORANGE   BROWN   BLUE   YELLOW   GREEN

Write down the total
you see in each row.

Let's see if your guess
was high or low.

49?

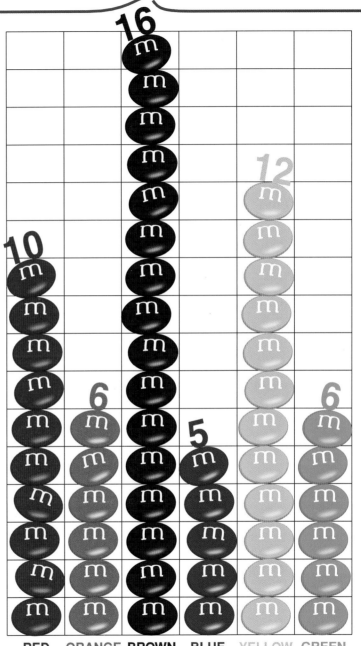

RED   ORANGE   BROWN   BLUE   YELLOW   GREEN

Add the numbers together.
The sum will be grand.

You can add the numbers
or count each candy by hand.

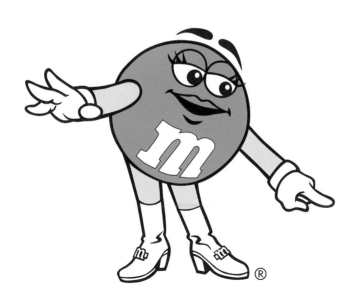

$$
\begin{array}{r}
10 \\
6 \\
16 \\
5 \\
12 \\
+ \ 6 \\
\hline
55
\end{array}
$$

Was the number you reached
more or less than you thought?

Take the small from the large.
That's the difference you've got.

$$\begin{array}{r} 4\ \overset{1}{\cancel{5}}5 \\ -\ 49 \\ \hline 6 \end{array}$$

You've worked very hard, so it's time for a treat.
Eat one of each color. That's six you can eat.

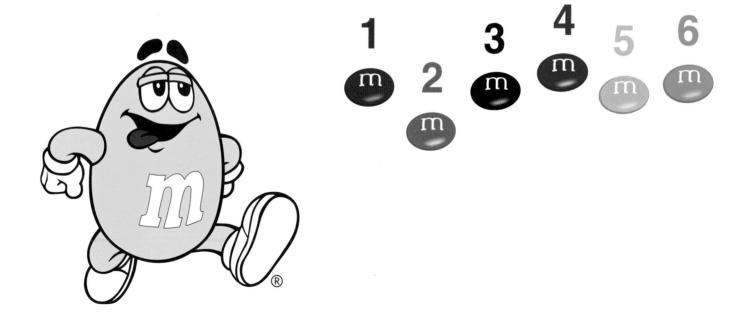

Push the candies together. Use these words as a guide.
Next we'll learn to multiply and divide.

It'll be easy to divide by two.
Let's do it like this: one for me, one for you.

Are the amounts unequal, or are they the same?
You'll find in division often one can "remain."

If you have a remainder,
you're not quite done.

Consider yourself lucky.
You get to eat one!

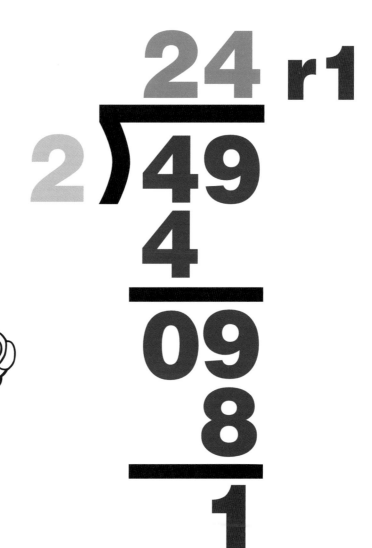

Split the two groups into four with ten in each bunch.
Any left over you should feel free to munch.

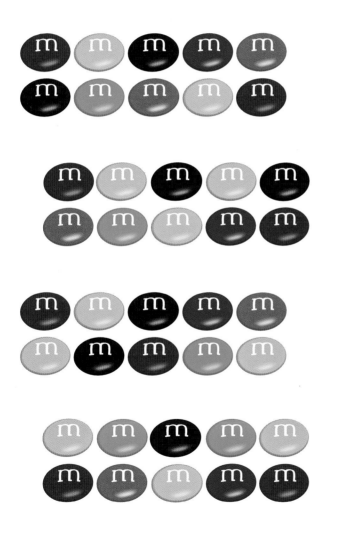

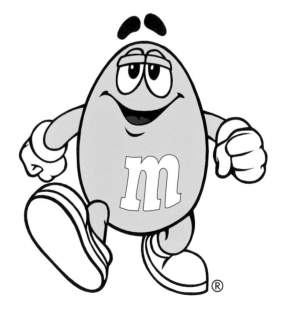

Four times ten is forty, as you can see.
Multiplying is easy if you look carefully.

4 x 10 = 40

Multiplying by ten can be fun, it's true.
Can you find the answer to ten times two?

10 x 2 = 20

If we turn it around, we get the same answer again.
Twenty's also the product of two times ten.

2 x 10 = 20

It's time now to change the four groups into eight.
If there are five in each group, you're doing just great!

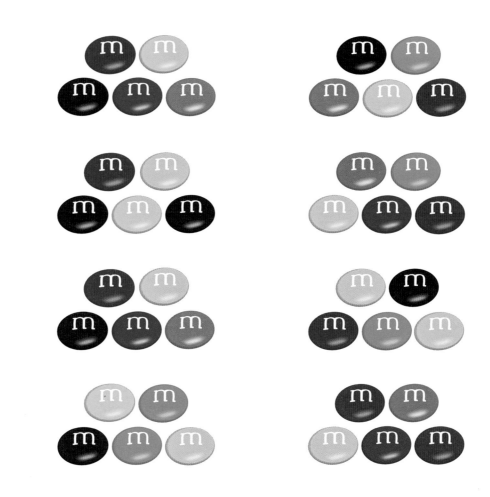

Count by fives up to forty, then it will be clear
what eight times five is. The answer's right here.

8 x 5 = 40

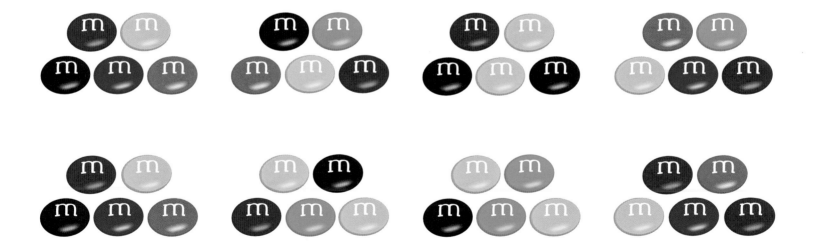

You have solved much, and you have learned plenty.
But do you know how many fives make up twenty?

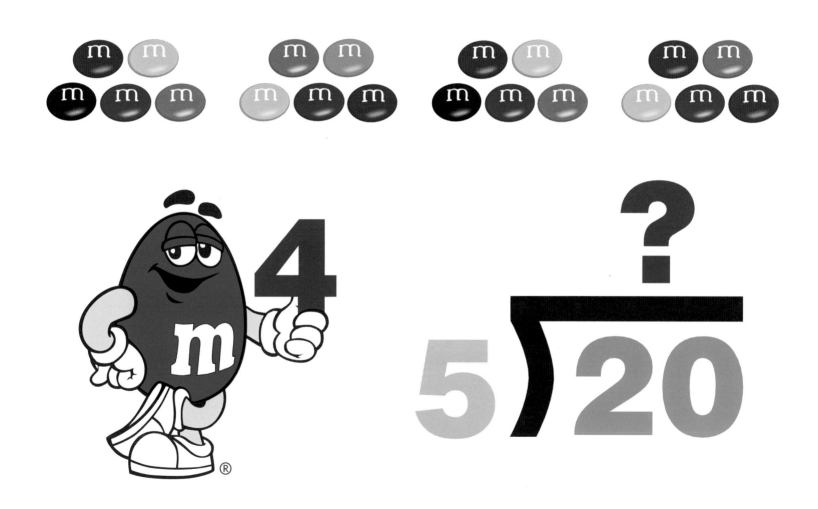

On the subject of twenty, we can do more.
You get the same number by making five groups of four.

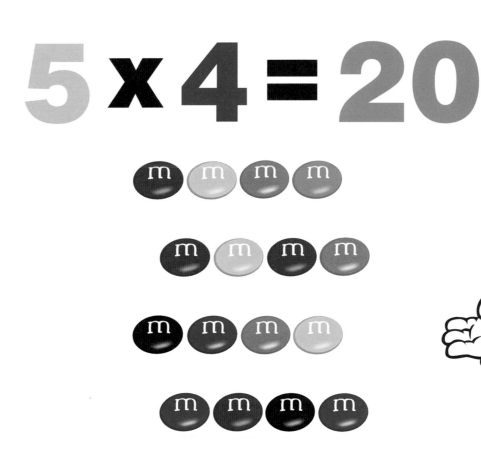

5 x 4 = 20

Take one of each color. Put them in a short line.
Start with your favorite. You're doing just fine.

The rest set aside and for now do not use.
Later divide them to share if you choose.

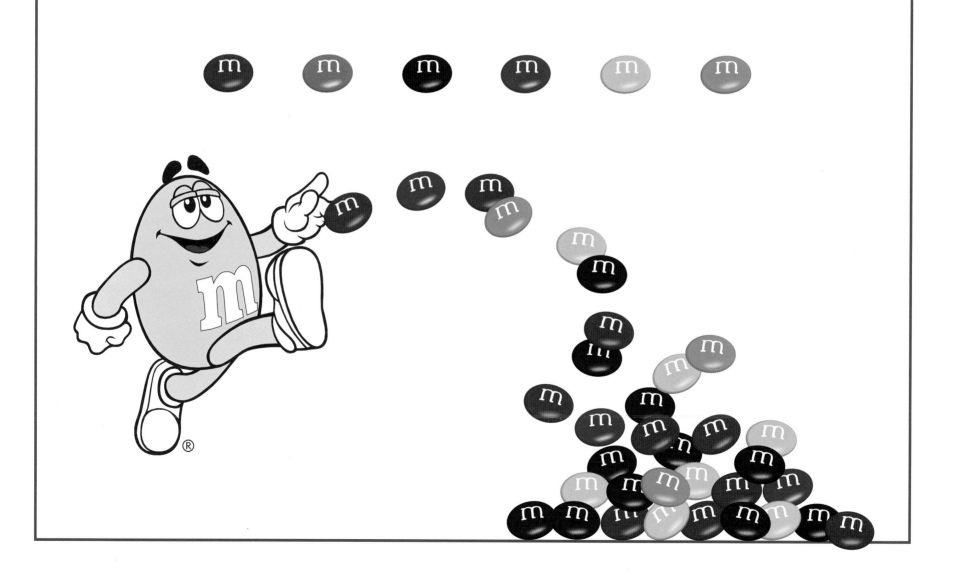

For the six that remain, slowly follow each word:
Eat the fourth first, the fifth second, and the third third!

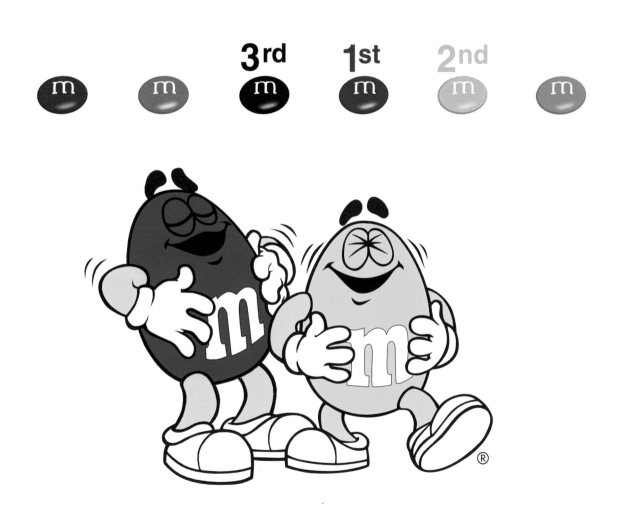

The second goes fourth. Its time has now passed.
The sixth will be fifth, and the first will be last.

6th 4th 3rd 1st 2nd 5th

Congratulations! Great job!
You're on the right path.

You followed directions
and had fun with math!

Here's a review so that you can look
at all the information you learned in this book.

Graphing

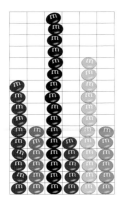

- Sort the candies by color
- Compare rows with the most and least
- Find equal rows
- Find the number of candies in each row
- Add the numbers or count the candies to find the total amount

Addition and Subtraction

$$
\begin{array}{r}
^{2}10 \\
6 \\
16 \\
5 \\
12 \\
+\quad 6 \\
\hline
55
\end{array}
\qquad
\begin{array}{r}
^{4\ 1}\!\!\!\!\not{5}\not{5} \\
-\ 49 \\
\hline
6
\end{array}
$$

Division

$$
\begin{array}{r}
24\ \text{r}1 \\
2\,\overline{)49} \\
4 \\
\hline
09 \\
8 \\
\hline
1
\end{array}
$$

Multiplication

$$2 \times 10 = 20$$

is the same as

$$10 \times 2 = 20$$

Ordinal Numbers

1st	2nd	3rd	4th	5th	6th